ANIMALS
ON THE EDGE

ENDANGERED

From tigers to polar bears and orangutans, all over the world animals are under real and immediate threat of extinction. Here we call them "Animals on the Edge".

LION
TIGER
CHEETAH
LEOPARD

Cats are nature's ultimate hunters. The famous five Big Cats are lion, tiger, leopard, jaguar and cheetah. Most live in jungles – jaguars in South America, tigers in Asia, but lions and cheetahs survive in the open plains of Africa. Lions use teamwork to bring down big grazers like wildebeest. Like an Olympic sprinter, the cheetah is a specialist and can only keep up its top speed of 65mph (105kmh) for short distances, so it has to catch its prey quickly – or go hungry!

BIG CATS

SIBERIAN TIGER

The largest cat in the world – but there may be fewer than 200 of these magnificent beasts left in the wild.

LEOPARD

Leopards, jaguars and panthers are all supreme jungle predators being extremely quick climbers and well camouflaged.

LION

The most social of wild cats, lions live in family groups called 'prides'.

CHEETAH

The fastest animal on the planet, a cheetah can accelerate from 0–60mph (0–97kmh) in 3 seconds – faster than many supercars!

In the past 20 years, the lion population in Africa has been reduced by half. Today less than 21,000 remain.

HIPPO
BEAR
BUFFALO
WILD WATER

WATER BUFFALO

In Asia, wild water buffalo are rare and in real danger of extinction. But the good news is that its domestic cousin is thriving and actually helping wildlife conservation.

POLAR BEAR

Polar bears, the world's largest land carnivores, have to be good swimmers — swimming between the sheets of ice in the Arctic when hunting for seals.

Most experts think grizzlies are the most aggressive of bears.

GRIZZLY BEAR

HIPPOPOTAMUS

Hippopotamuses are surprising animals. The closest living relatives to this large mammal are whales and dolphins. They may seem to be tame, but the hippopotamus is among the most dangerous and aggressive of all animals. More people are killed in Africa by hippos than by any other animal. Despite their short legs and round bodies, hippos can easily outrun humans reaching speeds of up to 30mph (50kmh)!

The largest of all brown bears are the grizzlies found on Kodiak Island, Alaska - they can grow up to 3m (10ft).

open these pages to see your ...

WILD ANIMAL 3-D

PANO

All American national parks, such as Yellowstone, have laws and regulations to protect the bears. This seems to be working and they are at a lower risk of extinction.

AFRICAN ELEPHANT

A trial of strength between two young bull (male) elephants...

...while the rest of the family group looks on.

INDIAN ELEPHANT

These Indian elephants enjoy cooling off after a hard day's work. They are often trained for heavy duty tasks like pulling timber.

ELEPHANT RHINO

THICK SKINS

Elephants are the largest land animals alive today. An average elephant grows to around 3.5m (11ft) at the shoulder and weighs in at around 6 tonnes. Living in family groups, these highly social mammals are very protective of other family members – especially young-sters. African elephants are usually slightly larger and have bigger ears and longer tusks than their Indian cousins.

3-D PANORAMA
ANIMALS
ON THE EDGE

Hunted to the point of extinction for their horns, African white rhinos now outnumber their leaf-eating relative, the black rhino. Rhinoceroses have sharp hearing and sense of smell, but very poor eyesight. Left alone in the wild, rhinos live to be about 60 years old or more.

RHINOCEROS

ANIMALS
ON THE EDGE

Elephants have always been hunted by poachers for their ivory tusks; now they are a protected species worldwide.

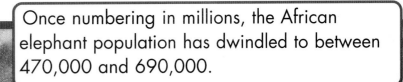
Once numbering in millions, the African elephant population has dwindled to between 470,000 and 690,000.

GORILLA

Almost 200 species of primates – including humans – live in the world today. All primates have five fingers and similar bodies. Another distinguishing feature is fingernails! Around two-thirds of today's primates are monkeys living in Asia, Africa and South America. Some, like the orangutan, demonstrate human characteristics such as laughter-like sounds and the ability to use objects as tools. The majority are vegetarian, but chimpanzees, for example, are known to kill monkeys for their meat.

An endangered forest dweller, the gorilla is the largest living primate and is one of man's closest relatives.

PRIMATES

GORILLA
ORANGUTAN
BABOON
MANDRILL

BABOON

Easily recognised by their 'dog-like' head shape, baboons live in large groups of females and youngsters and a single dominant male.

MANDRILL

A highly colourful species of baboon.

ORANGUTAN

Critically threatened in their native Sumatra and Borneo, orangutans are known for their high intelligence, very long arms and reddish-brown hair. Orangutans seem to enjoy physical contact and even laugh when tickled!

ANIMALS
ON THE EDGE

The two chimpanzee species, Common and Bonobo, are the closest living relatives to humans.

Chimpanzees rarely live past the age of 40 when they are in the wild, but they have been known to reach 60 in captivity.

SPEEDY GRAZERS

Animals have to be fast runners to survive on the African plains! They need to stay alert while looking for food and water. Lions, cheetahs and other predators plan surprise attacks on their next meal! Most grazing animals live in herds, relying on the senses of their fellow grazers to warn of danger. Grazing animals are a very important part of the plains ecosystem. Their waste fertilizes the soil, their grazing and trampling encourage new growth and without regular cropping, the grassland would soon become overgrown.

WILDEBEEST

Wildebeest are famous for a mass migration in May when 1.5 million move to new feeding grounds.

GAZELLE

Thomson's gazelle, often affectionately known as a 'tommy', has a unique bounding leap.